CO-DVX-928

the birth date book

This Book Belongs to

_____

The Birth Date Book

May 8

What Your Birth Date Reveals about You

Julie Mars

Illustrated by Claude Martinot

Ariel Books

Andrews McMeel Publishing

Kansas City

www.andrewsmcmeel.com

ISBN: 0-8362-6048-1

Series editor: Sue Carnahan
Series design by Junie Lee
Typesetting by Nina Gaskin

CONTENTS

introduction

Your birth date is more than just a passing squiggle on the calendar, more than an excuse to exceed your daily calorie ration. Your birth date is a *fateful* day; a day where the forces of the universe came together in a unique way to chart your destiny; a moment in time imprinted on your very being. Who you are, where you've been, where you're headed—all of these things had their beginning on the month, day, and hour of your birth.

The Birth Date Book sheds some light

on these influences and offers a series of snapshots of who you are. Are you glamorous and outgoing like Cindy Crawford, coolly buttoned-down like Sidney Poitier, or an unpredictable mixture of the two? Why do you prefer a particular color, taste, or scent? What career paths appeal to you? Do you harbor a secret vocation in esoteric anthropology, or does crunching numbers send you into paroxysms of joy? What about your home? Is it styled with the spacious calm of a

Zen monastery or riotously festooned like a Jamaican nightclub? Who can inspire you to drop everything and go to the ends of the earth? And who sends you running lickety-split for the nearest exit?

You'll find both surprising *and* familiar answers to these questions in the following pages. Consider this book a toast to your special day—and to the exceptional being that you are now, and continue to become every day of your life.

your astrological

sun sign

TAURUS

Taurus the Bull is astrologically famous for two very different things: sultry sensuality and a red-hot temper. Ruled by the planet Venus, the goddess of love and fertility, Taurus thrives in a beautiful, peaceful environment. You are known for your lazily amorous inclinations and your deep appreciation of the "now" as opposed to the past or future. Each of your five senses is highly developed, resulting in a person that's, at best, artistic and gentle, and at worst, self-indulgent and passive.

Like the bull, you tend to be slow-moving, persistent, and steadfast. You can also be stubborn to the point of rigidity. You are slow to anger, but if you're pushed, watch out! When Taurus sees red, everybody else should head for cover.

Taureans prefer their familiar world and tend to be suspicious of outside influences. Calm, conservative, and slightly materialistic, the average Taurus builds an idyllic home life and defends it with vigor.

Remember, your key words "I have" do not imply any cause for insecurity, so don't hold on too tight. You must step carefully around these Taurean pitfalls in order to enjoy your particular birthright—a life filled with the rare capacity to be supremely happy and fulfilled in the moment.

your personal
tarot card

THE WORLD

The World is the twenty-first card of the Major Arcana, the twenty-two most powerful cards in the tarot deck. This joyful image of fruition symbolizes the completion of a journey through life, and depicts your soul as part of a larger whole . . . a never-ending circle of birth and rebirth. The World suggests that you've found where you belong . . . but you could still use a vacation every now and then!

your chinese astrological symbol

Your sign comes around only once every twelve years in the Chinese zodiac, but during that year your number will definitely come up a winner in the cosmic lottery. Each sign is governed by the qualities of a particular animal guardian. Are you patient as an ox? Wise as a snake? Vain as a monkey? Locate the year of your birth in the chart below to find out—if you dare.

THE YEAR OF THE RAT

1900, 1912, 1924, 1936, 1948, 1960, 1972, 1984, 1996

Popular, ambitious, honest, and stubborn

THE YEAR OF THE OX

1901, 1913, 1925, 1937, 1949, 1961, 1973, 1985, 1997

Patient, strong, original, and rigid

THE YEAR OF THE TIGER

1902, 1914, 1926, 1938, 1950, 1962, 1974, 1986, 1998

Generous, noble, passionate, and hotheaded

THE YEAR OF THE RABBIT

1903, 1915, 1927, 1939, 1951, 1963, 1975, 1987, 1999

Discreet, sensitive, clever, and devious

THE YEAR OF THE DRAGON

1904, 1916, 1928, 1940, 1952, 1964, 1976, 1988, 2000

Enthusiastic, intuitive, shrewd, and demanding

THE YEAR OF THE SNAKE

1905, 1917, 1929, 1941, 1953, 1965, 1977, 1989, 2001

Wise, compassionate, elegant, and extravagant

THE YEAR OF THE HORSE

1906, 1918, 1930, 1942, 1954, 1966, 1978, 1990, 2002

Independent, hardworking, charming, and rebellious

THE YEAR OF THE GOAT

1907, 1919, 1931, 1943, 1955, 1967, 1979, 1991, 2003

Creative, tasteful, lovable, and fickle

THE YEAR OF THE MONKEY

1908, 1920, 1932, 1944, 1956, 1968, 1980, 1992, 2004

Witty, nimble, passionate, and vain

THE YEAR OF THE ROOSTER

1909, 1921, 1933, 1945, 1957, 1969, 1981, 1993, 2005

Frank, talented, industrious, and pompous

THE YEAR OF THE DOG

1910, 1922, 1934, 1946, 1958, 1970, 1982, 1994, 2006

Loyal, modest, intelligent, and pessimistic

THE YEAR OF THE PIG

1911, 1923, 1935, 1947, 1959, 1971, 1983, 1995, 2007

Honest, sociable, cultured, and gullible

crowning jewel

EMERALD

The brilliant green emerald is more than a stone: It's the acknowledged symbol of creativity, abundance, and fertility of mind and body. When you wear an emerald, you embody the creative force of Mother Nature herself. As if that's not enough, it's the only precious gem in which the flaws are considered assets—a distinction that often applies to you, the wearer, as well!

lucky number

TWENTY-ONE

Twenty-one is the number of mastery. You are fully, happily, and enthusiastically immersed in the dance of existence while simultaneously fulfilling each of your responsibilities. Your life is a monument to self-discipline, with a great sense of humor as a primary building block. The result is a winning combination— a just reward for your years of diligent "self-construction"!

alphabet soup

C, D, and P

May 8s often find that names and places beginning with the following letters become especially significant during the course of their lives: *C, D,* and *P.* With your *conscientiousness,* command of *detail,* and *practicality,* you can build an empire wherever you happen to be . . . and enjoy controlling it! But relaxation and fun are also part of your reward, so celebrate!

week link

SUNDAY

The magnificent Sun, giver of all life and source of all energy and nourishment in our system, rules your significant day of the week. Like the Sun, you have the potential to shine in any situation. Use your personal day of power to bring positivity and healing energy to all those around you! They will certainly appreciate basking in your Sun-day brilliance!

your magical food

CARROTS

Carrots. Kids like their crunch; models like their calories; Bugs Bunny just likes them. So it is with May 8s. People are drawn to you for all kinds of reasons. Besides your accessibility and easygoing nature, you are as trustworthy as a person can be. You're everybody's friend and nobody's enemy. One in a million, that's you.

your color cue

SCARLET

Redder than red, hotter than hot, scarlet is a passionate color. Just as scarlet is intense, so are you. Tempering your emotions probably never occurs to you, particularly when it's so much more satisfying (and fun) to go over the top! May 8s often love with more passion, eat with greater gusto, and suffer with sharper pain than anyone else.

flower power

COLUMBINE

Graceful as the columbine, tender and tenderhearted, May 8s can nearly always soothe an aching head or comfort a breaking heart. Empathetic by nature, you know by instinct when to offer assistance and, equally important, when to back off. But let's not get too serious! You can be a healer, yes, but first things first: Where's the party?

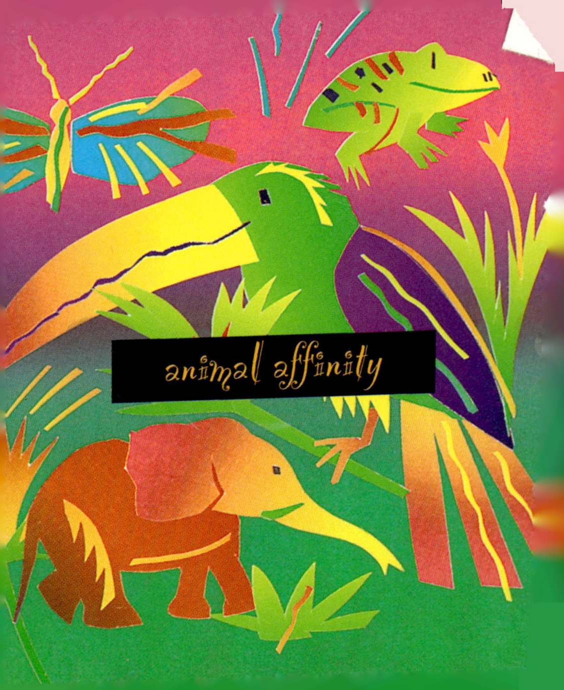
animal affinity

MONKEY

The monkey confidently swings through the trees, chattering up a storm and tumbling like a trained acrobat. It is wildly energetic, clever, and mischievous . . . and beloved for its antics! May 8s, too, are much appreciated for their cleverness, enthusiasm, and ingenuity. You get the job done—and keep everyone entertained while doing it!

your first desire

ELEGANCE

An eye for beauty and an appreciation of culture and luxury—these elements combine to create a typical May 8. Because you are so enchanted by refinement, your first desire is pure, old-fashioned elegance. In your future there's a highly polished dance floor—and you are ready and willing to tango!

your secret wish

May 8s are reliable, responsible, dependable . . . and frequently taken for granted. This truly irks you, but your basic self-respect forbids you to stamp your feet and yell, "Me! Me! Me!" Deep within, though, your secret wish is to be not only noticed but also praised. More than one friend would agree that you deserve that wish!

personality profile

Can a romantic and sentimental spirit survive in a practical, commonsensical body? Can a person with an easygoing, gentle temperament suddenly snap, snort, and charge like an angry, Taurean bull? Can a careful, placid individual build a charmed life of luxury and comfort?

The typical May 8 may give surprising answers: Yes! Yes! Yes!

Perhaps it's your overall earthiness that allows you to mix and match personality traits that seem to be at odds with each other. Or perhaps it's the result of your patience and understanding. Whatever the reason, May 8s can do it seamlessly! You are mysteriously able to remain a happy creature of habit and simultaneously whip up a world of spontaneous passion.

Stability, perseverance, and loyalty are frequently the characteristics most closely associated with May 8s. You tend to make friendships in kindergarten that last a lifetime, and no one is surprised to see you start off in the company mailroom and end up in the executive suite. Once you get there, you hold on tightly to your well-deserved laurels. May 8s definitely enjoy being at the top of the pecking order, yet they tend to remain open, easygoing, and friendly toward all.

May 8s usually combine creativity and endurance in precisely the right proportions. If you truly desire to produce perfect, trout-fishing flies, a hand-carved dining room table, or even the great American novel, you have the discipline and drive to *just do it!* And since you're usually a perfectionist, you won't quit until you earn your own personal seal of approval.

Because you tend to demand the biggest bang for the buck, you are able to spot a bargain—and get it for even less! You might need to visit four different megastores for all the components, but when you're done, your sound system will rival the one at the trendiest hot spot—for a fraction of the cost. And you will definitely relax and enjoy it, perhaps with a few close friends.

While May 8s are often viewed as conservative and serious, they are just as frequently described by close friends and family as serene and uninhibited. You wear such labels with quiet confidence. Secure in yourself, the world, and maybe even the universe, May 8s are built to endure—and to enjoy every single minute!

room for improvement

You understand and respect money, but sometimes, May 8s' unwillingness to part with it gets out of hand. If you notice a sudden change of attitude among your friends when you grab the bill to figure out your precise percentage, down to the last penny, it's probably because you're falling into the dreaded category marked "tightwad." Loosen up! Throw in the extra fifty cents! It will be good for your soul!

This May 8 determination to do *exactly* what's required, no more and no less, sometimes spreads into the realms of behavior, action, and attitude too. Your resistance to change is a source of comfort to you, but it can also be an unnecessary limitation. You may always know where you're headed, but if you vary your route, you may discover an intriguing new world . . . not very far from your own beaten tracks!

Experiment and try a different coffee shop in the morning. If that's too unsettling, order the blueberry pancakes instead of the cheddar cheese omelette. From time immemorial, the wisest people have known that variety is the spice of life. May 8s sometimes need to be gently reminded!

May 8s tend to thoroughly relish free time and luxurious surroundings. But sometimes you get a bit *too* comfortable, and you may neglect matters that shouldn't be ignored. Don't allow yourself to drift into a permanent state of inertia—a May 8 pitfall! Remember, activity makes those delicious periods of leisure truly peak experiences!

on the job

When a project requires meticulous planning, long-term endurance, and a cool head for the duration . . . a May 8 is the best bet! You typically thrive on a meaty challenge, and you have both the necessary passion *and* patience. As long as there is one last i to dot or one last t to cross, May 8s are on the case . . . but the very second the job is done, they sit back, put their feet up, call for a cold drink, and celebrate!

Because you have a nurturing, calm personality, you may frequently find yourself in the role of mentor. Add to that your stamina, and the sky's the limit as far as interesting workplace possibilities. Perhaps you will lead a group of city slickers through an Outward Bound survival training course or supervise a science laboratory where results are measured by an electron microscope!

Whatever the venue, typical May 8s have the sharp eyes of eagles—and are able to see hazards in advance and smoothly sidestep obstacles on the road to success.

Occasionally you are accused of being bullheaded. You tend to straddle the fine line between obstinacy and the authoritative voice of experience. Remember, if you tone it down a little, the result will be the same and the work environment will be that much more pleasant.

May 8s' attention to detail, persistence, and dependability define them as major workplace assets. And you tend to have both the salary and the savings account to prove to yourself just how valuable you really are!

at play

A rock-climbing expedition, an antique show, a professional basketball game—May 8s are likely to be on hand for any of them. And because you typically have limitless energy for amusement, you may attend them all on the same weekend!

You tend to be most comfortable in a group of friends, and because you are so often an excellent planner, the responsibility for filling the social calendar often falls to you. May 8s might search for the most outlandish pastime and have no trouble convincing others that a day trip to the birthplace of some eccentric front-porch philosopher will be a major hoot! And it will—because you have the Midas touch when it comes to recreation.

But May 8s typically have a domestic streak as well, so spending an evening at home with the latest bestseller or a stack of videos from the golden age of Hollywood is more than satisfying. You've even been known to personally revive the ancient (and increasingly lost) art of letter writing! Your correspondence might be destined for the mailbox of your local newspaper . . . or the U.S. senator from your district. Whatever your cause, you will doggedly pursue it to your satisfaction!

Your creativity finds many outlets in your free-time activities. Whether it's karaoke or kayaking, May 8s are at the forefront of fun—and on the lookout for even more!

home sweet home

For many May 8s, the home is a combination refuge, workplace, and artwork-in-progress. Your goal is likely a combination of peace, comfort, beauty, and efficiency. Consequently, decorating decisions are often monumental for May 8s.

You may carry tiles in three shades of blue in your pocket for weeks, trying to choose the one that's absolutely perfect for your new kitchen counter, or you may spend two hours in a music store, carefully considering which blues CD would go best with breakfast.

Whatever the whim, it's all a part of the slice of Shangri-la May 8s call home.

May 8s want their homes to reflect a mix of their own past history, present interests, and future goals. You may proudly use your championship trophy for the hundred-yard dash won in the eighth grade as a paperweight for your master's degree thesis notes or display your personal five-year plan on the refrigerator door for all to see. You use your abode as a base of operations *and* a rest ranch. Your home serves both purposes in exactly the right proportions.

Friends, family, and significant others are of great importance to you, and you make ample room for all in both your home and your daily life. Because they tend to enjoy cooking, many May 8s host the annual Thanksgiving feast *and* the New Year's celebration. Your home remains a favorite spot—partially due to its warmth and comfort, but mostly because *you* are in it!

how do you love?

The May 8 approach to life in general is conservative, careful, and more than a little stubborn. And when it comes to love and romance, you tend to be *at least* twice as cautious as others are! May 8s will spend a great deal of time in the search for precisely the right partner, rarely losing hope, and rarely settling for less than the ideal they seek. And once you find that person, you tend to hold on for dear life!

This possessiveness merely reflects the time you may have waited for true love. Because you know value—and demand it—you simply must protect it (though occasionally May 8s perceive threats to their bliss where there are none).

When your partner feels the leash is too short, it's time to loosen your grip. Rely on your passionate, magnetic nature to cast the spell that will put a restless partner at ease. The sensuality of a May 8 is like a natural hot spring on a cold day . . . irresistible! Use it! It's more effective than a steaming cup of hot chocolate and a fuzzy blanket when your partner wants to be warmed up a bit!

When it comes to longevity in relationships, May 8s score in the top percentiles. Because home life, family, and romance create a desirable environment for you, you thrive within the institutions of long-term love and commitment. And the good news is, your passionate nature is like a rare flower that continues to bloom, in bright and surprising colors year after year.

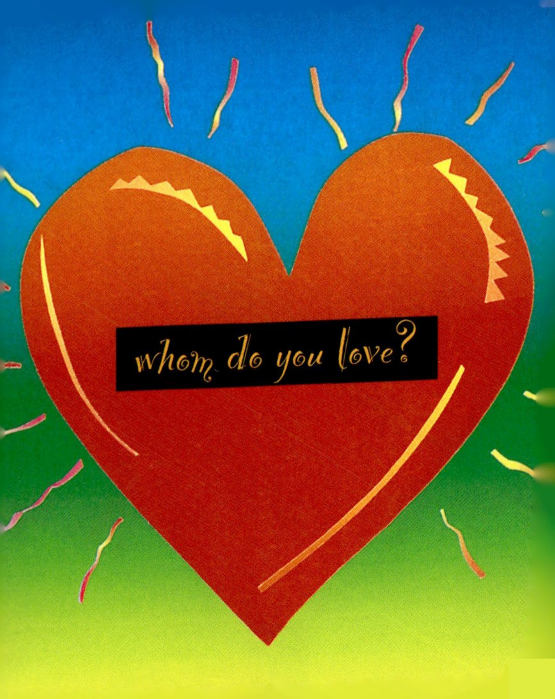
whom do you love?

May 8s (Taurus) get along best with:

Taurus (April 21–May 21)
Cancer (June 22–July 23)
Virgo (August 24–September 23)
Sagittarius
    (November 23–December 21)
Capricorn
    (December 22–January 20)
Pisces (February 20–March 20)

May 8s (Taurus) get along better without:

Aries (March 21–April 20)
Gemini (May 22–June 21)
Leo (July 24–August 23)
Libra (September 24–October 23)
Scorpio (October 24–November 22)
Aquarius (January 21–February 19)

M ay 8s seek out people who are:

faithful, talkative, patient, loyal, acquisitive, and hardworking.

M ay 8s avoid people who are:

pushy, impulsive, eccentric, analytical, independent, or casual about love.

famous/infamous people born today

Don Rickles (1926) stand-up comedian

Edward Gibbon (1737) historian,
The History of the Decline and Fall of the Roman Empire

Roberto Rossellini (1906) film director,
Open City

Alex Van Halen (1955) drummer, Van Halen, "Jump"

Harry S Truman (1884) thirty-third president of the United States

Rick Nelson (1940) singer, "Travelin'
  Man"

Edmund Wilson (1895) critic and
  essayist, *To the Finland Station*

Sonny Liston (1917) world heavyweight
  boxing champion

Melissa Gilbert (1964) actress, *Little
  House on the Prairie*

Keith Jarrett (1945) jazz pianist and
  composer

Thomas Pynchon (1937) novelist,
  Gravity's Rainbow

Gary Snyder (1930) Beat movement
  poet, *Turtle Island;* ecological activist

oh what a day it was

MAY 8

Coca-Cola goes on sale for the first time, in Atlanta; it's sold as a remedy for headaches and hangovers (1886)

First use of electric starting gate in horse racing, at Hollywood Park, Inglewood, California (1939)

Cartoon character Alfred E. Neuman appears on the cover of *Mad* magazine for the first time (1956)

flashback: your past lives

In any past life, May 8s would have been in close connection to the earth —or its symbolic equivalent, the world of practicality. It is not unlikely that your past lives included the following occupations:

> Gemologist
> Surveyor
> Organic farmer
> Beekeeper
> Shepherd
> Mason

your personal proverb

The face is the portrait of the mind;
the eyes, its informers.

Latin proverb